M000031380

GAINING *a*
LEASH *on* LIFE

Lessons From Bud

GAINING *a*
LEASH *on* LIFE

Lessons From Bud

RICHARD D. PARSONS, PHD

Willow Creek Press

© 2006 Richard D. Parsons
All Illustrations © Virginia Morton

All rights reserved. No part of this book may be reproduced or
transmitted in any form by any means, electronic or mechanical,
including photocopying, recording, or by any information
storage and retrieval system, without written permission from the
Publisher.

Published by Willow Creek Press
P.O. Box 147, Minocqua, Wisconsin 54548

Editor: Andrea K. Donner
Design: Amy Kolberg

Library of Congress Cataloging-in-Publication Data

Parsons, Richard D.
  Gaining a leash on life : lessons from Bud / Richard D. Parsons.
    p. cm.
  ISBN 1-59543-446-1 (hardcover : alk. paper)
  1. Dogs--Miscellanea. 2. Conduct of life. I. Title.
  SF426.2.P38 2006
  158.1--dc22
                                    2006024314

DEDICATION

To all the....
Bud's, Happy's, Bailey's, Gus's,
Spunkies, Jake's, Saki's, Zeke's, Henry's, and...
If we only could be the people
you thought us to be!

*In order to really enjoy a dog, one doesn't
merely try to train him to be semi-human.
The point is to open oneself to the possibility
of becoming partly a dog.*

—Edward Hoagland

Contents

Foreword

(You don't have to own a dog to learn lessons from a Bud!)

Well, it was two A.M. for goodness sake, and I thought, "What could he possibly be howling at?" I stumbled from my bed expecting to see an intruder at my window or one of our world's creatures invading our domain. I found neither. I found only my dog Bud—howling—with all the vigor that his 14 years would allow. Yep, there he sat, almost nobly, howling at the moon. A moon so bright that you would think it was summoning the morning crow.

Watching him seemed to touch something deep within me... something, that I had almost forgotten. So, I sat beside him and for a brief moment, I howled along with him!

Now you need to understand that howling is not something that comes easily to me. My experience as a psychologist, a university professor, and an author of over 50 books and articles has led me to believe that anything as frivolous as a two A.M. howl need simply be avoided. And yet that same experience—especially the 27 years of working in clinical practice with many individuals who found themselves struggling with life stressors—has helped me to realize that it is exactly these types of things—these two A.M. howls—which are not only NOT frivolous, but may be life saving.

Even with all that we have to do and all the real concerns of life in the 21st century, the reasons and opportunities to howl remain, and the benefits cannot be denied. *Gaining a Leash on Life* is a book for all of us who could benefit from learning a new way of embracing life. It is a book for all of us who can lament that we "howl" less than we would like. Learning to howl, in all it's glory, is really what this book is all about.

Learning from Bud

The fact that our canine friends can teach us lessons about life has been well documented not only in the journals and in the hearts of every dog lover, but documented in and through the world of science. In a study reported in the April, 2002, issue of *Prevention* magazine, 48 New York stockbrokers with hypertension were given medication. In addition to this medicine, half also adopted a pet. After six months, the resting blood pressure of all the stock brokers had dropped. But when all the stockbrokers

The journey to gain a leash on life begins.

were under stress, *only* the new pet owners had blood pressure in the normal range. Other studies have demonstrated that companion dogs can reduce the healing time of patients with serious illness, shorten bereavement, and can improve overall health.

Dogs have also been found to do as much for our spirits and our emotions as they do for our bodies. As far back as 1792, dogs were used in the treatment of mental patients at York Retreat, England. In 1919, the U.S. Secretary of the Interior suggested to the superintendent of St. Elizabeth's Hospital in Washington, D.C., that dogs be used as companions for psychiatric patients. The research suggests that the unconditional love provided by our canine companions is healing, to both body and soul.

But dogs are more that just good medicine. Dogs are more than wonderful companions. They are, or can be, master teachers and in many ways models who show us how to live. If we allow our canine friends to simply show the way, we may learn the valuable life lessons they already have mastered. Lessons such as:

- When loved ones come home, always run to greet them like they've been gone for a year.

- Never pass up the opportunity to go for a joyride in the car.

- Allow the experience of fresh air and the wind in your face to be pure ecstasy.
- When it's in your best interest, practice obedience.
- Let others know when they've invaded your territory.
- Take naps.
- Stretch before rising.
- Run, romp, and play daily.
- Thrive on attention and let people touch you.
- Avoid biting when a simple growl will do.
- When you're happy, dance around and wiggle your entire body.

It is these and so many other valuable lessons about life that we can learn if we simply allow our canine companions to show the way. It is these lessons, these *'dogmas'* that will help each of us *gain a leash on life*. And it is these lessons that are presented within this book.

About this Book

Gaining a Leash on Life is more than a book. *Gaining a Leash on Life* is an invitation and a guide. Throughout the upcoming pages you will be invited to gain a new

Howling is good for the soul.

perspective. As you read, you will be guided through a series of steps all aimed at helping you increase your awareness and acceptance of self, of others, and the world in which you live. As a result of this new perspective, you will become... more whole... more authentic. And, with this new perspective, you will realize that you, like both Bud and I, have ample reason "to howl" and to celebrate life.

Gaining a Leash on Life is organized around four themes: Awareness, Acceptance, Authenticity, and Celebration. Within each of these themes, you will find a number of lessons, or what I call "Dog-mas." Now, these dog-mas are not *dogma* and as such they are not meant to be read as 'rigid' truths but rather as a new perspective from which to view and experience your life. Each of the dog-mas opens with a quote, which I hope will stimulate your thought and reflection. The dog-ma is explained and my reflections on the topic are shared.

But as you most likely know, actually gaining a leash on life requires more than reading and reflecting. It requires *doing,* and doing *differently!* Therefore at the end of each of the dog-mas I have presented a series of guides, or recommendations, called "Bud-isms" (directives from my best Bud-dog). These Bud-isms will help you to embrace the invitation found within the dog-ma and translate them into actions and life decisions.

As you take time to experiment with the Bud-ism and further reflect on the dog-mas, you will come to appreciate that these are things that are best savored, not rushed through. This book it is not meant to be approached as a task with a deadline, or as a process with the goal of completion. More than a typical book, *Gaining a Leash on Life* is intended to serve as an experience from which you will emerge with a different, and hopefully, rewarding perspective on yourself, others, and the world around you.

It is my hope that you find this book to be a welcome companion as you journey through your year. It is also my hope that as you read and reflect you will more fully appreciate the truth, that while "Dogs are not our whole life... they make our lives whole." (Roger Caras).

About Bud

I am sure if I asked my dog what I should write as a way of introduction, he would instruct me to write simply that he is.... Bud! Bud is less concerned and certainly not encumbered by details. I am sure he feels it is inconsequential that he is 14 years old and an SPCA mix of terrier and an amalgam of friendly dogs. He may question the value of you knowing that his hair, which was once shiny black, has moved beyond salt and pepper to mostly salt. Nor would he need you to know that he moves a tad slower and with a bit more pain in the joints than he once did.

No, Bud would just want you to know that he is—Bud. His owner (that's me) would want you to know that Bud is a gift—a wonder—a love. But I'm sure as you read on, this is something you will soon come to understand.

Section I
Awareness

Your diamonds are not in far distant
mountains or in yonder seas;
they are in your own backyard,
if you dig for them.

—Russell Conwell

It has gotten to the point that whenever I am contemplating taking Bud for a walk, any preparation such as getting my sneakers or finding his leash needs to be done secretively. The mere mention of the word "walk," or the sight of his leash, throws him into uncontrollable excitement and apparent euphoria.

As soon as he sees his leash, or sees me putting on my sneakers, Bud starts to jump up and down, as if I were offering him a treat. He'll move to the door and then back to me, each time becoming all the more excited. And if I delay too long in getting my shoes on, he will nuzzle me with his nose, which when accompanied by a bark, signals, "Okay... let's get going!"

To be quite honest, I don't completely get it. I mean, why all the exuberance? After all, he has a nice back yard and we take walks pretty regularly. So what's the big deal? I mean, it's *only* a walk.

Well, I guess that is true for me. It is only a walk. It is a walk that I have done many times. It is a walk around a path in the neighborhood that has been well worn by our travels and which offers sights and sounds that I can predict before their arrival. But that's me.

Bud, on the other hand, seems to be aware of something that I am missing. For Bud, there is no such thing as *only* a walk. For that matter, there is no such thing as *only* 'a' ride, or 'a' treat, or 'a' visitor or even 'a' game of rough housing. No, Bud seems to take each of these events and all his other daily experiences as things to be savored. He seems to approach each experience as if it were for the first time. Bud, apparently, is aware of the prize, the richness, the diamond that each of these *only* experiences actually has to offer.

If you are like me, it has been too long since the simple daily events in your life were viewed as diamonds. The gifts to be unearthed by our daily walks often go undiscovered. For many of us, the beauty and the opportunity that surrounds us, each day of our lives, has too often gone unnoticed. It is easy to miss these diamonds in our own backyards when our vision is set only on far off shores. Rushing from one deadline to the next, or moving from the completion of one task only to begin again, steals us from the moment, *this* moment in which there are diamonds to be found.

What does it take to unearth the specialness of our moments? Nothing so difficult… just simple awareness! While there are many new tools—new ways of viewing our life—that we can use to unearth, polish, and enjoy our findings, the first, and perhaps the most essential tool is that of simple AWARENESS.

The joy of once buried treasures.

Maybe that seems too simple. I mean, after all, aren't we already aware? I am sure you function without banging into things, getting lost, or being unable to identify who you are, where you are, and what you are doing. How much more aware could you, or should you, be?

Hopefully, as you read through this section with its dog-mas and Bud-isms you will be able to answer that question for yourself. But even before you do—just consider how many times you have gone through your day almost 'mindlessly'? You know, drift through the morning coffee, the paper, and maybe a perfunctory conversation with another. Perhaps you traveled to work on a path so well worn that you often find yourself needing to "snap out of it" once you've arrived at your destination. Are you really aware? Were you aware of all that is invading your senses? Were you aware of the opportunities, the invitations that were offered? Were you aware of all the options, the subtle choices, the personal values that were operating at any one moment?

If you are like me, the answer will most likely be "no." And, if you are like me, the "dog-mas" found within this section will not only help you to become more aware, but will help you to find the diamonds in your own back yard.

Dog-ma 1:
The Dog-ma of Your Uniqueness

I'm a lean dog, a keen dog, a wild dog, and lone;
I'm a rough dog, a tough dog, hunting on my own;
I'm a bad dog, a mad dog, teasing silly sheep;
I love to sit and bay the moon to keep fat souls from sleep.

—Irene MacLeod

D o you think dogs worry about their coats not being as shiny as another's? Do you think they feel a bit of shame if their hair is a bit too wild? Do you think that dogs spend their free time worrying whether other dogs like them? Of course not.

It seems that unlike our four-footed friends, our own desire to fit in, to be accepted, to keep up with the Jones', Smith's, or whomever, often takes center stage and, in fact, *robs* us. Our desires and aspirations to be "just like Mike," or Mom, or the person next door, while fostering our dreams, can rob us from the joy of knowing the *uniqueness* of (our)*self*.

If you have ever observed a lean, swift dog running down the beach, along the edge of the water—timing her leap perfectly to grab the falling Frisbee—you know what a wondrous sight it is. But, even when such leanness or such athleticism is absent, there is wonder to be found in observing your pooch. Sure, the grace of our Frisbee catchers is something to celebrate, but so is watching the somewhat aged, overweight hound roll over in response to his owner's command. The wonder, the beauty of these two experiences rests not so much in the specific achievement displayed, but rather simply in the uniqueness of each dog. The hound, so content with his 'roll over' success, is no less proud than our leaping Frisbee catcher. And for us, the prize, the diamond to be grasped at this moment, is simply in our own awareness of each dog, simply doing his or her own thing, and doing it like no other!

Not all of us are or want to be Frisbee catchers. We don't need to be. Perhaps you are not athletic or gifted at music or art. Perhaps your mechanical abilities are less than magical and your cooking skills still seek refinement. Perhaps you find your talents lay elsewhere. It doesn't matter. The diamonds lay not so much in your ability to perform these tasks, nor even in the specific gift or talent you may display. The true diamonds lay in your awareness and appreciation of that which are *your* gifts, *your* talents. With this awareness you will under-

Celebrating simple joys.

stand that just like our friends the rolling hound or the leaping Frisbee catcher, that it is simply in doing what is *you* where your diamonds will be found.

There is a wonderful story told by Martin Buber, the great Jewish philosopher, about an enlightened master, Rabbi Zusya. The Rabbi, in reflecting upon his use of his talents pondered: "If they ask me in the next world, 'Why were you not Moses?' I will know the answer. But if they ask me, 'Why were you not Zusya?' I will have nothing." How will you answer that question?

To be "you" is a gift. The uniqueness of any one person is certainly wondrous. There is magic in our individuality. Think about it. Only you have those exact chromosomes... and only you have walked in those shoes for these many years. Uniqueness! What a gift. Why not unwrap it?

The first step to un-wrapping this gift of "you" and unearthing the diamonds within is to become more *aware* of the person you are, with all your talents and limitations, all of your "you-ness." I am not talking about simply noticing. When we notice, we see the superficial. We see the hair which is not just right or the pounds we've gained (or lost), or we may even focus on the award we won, or that special skill we possess. These are important but these are only hints of the "you" yet to be discovered. So as you proceed, don't get lost in the pimples or the dimples—just open yourself to the experience and awareness of you and your world.

A Bud-ism: Lesson on Uniqueness

Perhaps you, like many of us, have for too long been concerned about blending in whenever and wherever you can. And perhaps now, upon reflection, you can identify times that fitting in—blending in—came at the expense of your uniqueness. There certainly is nothing wrong with wanting to belong. But belonging only really works when you belong as you... not as a shell of you being someone else. So the current lessons from Bud are aimed at increasing your awareness of how you stand out—how you are different, unique—You! When you are aware, you can continue to give shape and form to this you—and celebrate in the process.

Taking Time to Observe

Did you ever wonder what a naturalist such as Charles Darwin would write, if *you* were the object of his observations? You might be surprised. Granted, you 'see' yourself everyday, in many situations, and maybe even in every way... but have you really taken time to truly focus on *you*. Have really taken the time to observe yourself and to begin to see that which is uniquely you? If not, now is a great time to start.

Observing the Physical You

- Take note of the uniqueness of your body—its symmetry and asymmetry.

- Take time in the morning, before rushing to dress for your busy day, to observe the rich shades and textures that are you. This is not a time to evaluate, just observe and be aware.

- Find opportunity to observe the features of your face—the design of your hand—that while showing similarity to a parent or grandparent continues to remain one of a kind.

- Observe your pattern of breath, and characteristics of your stride; they are often the announcements of your arrival even before others see you.

Observing the Social You

- Be aware of your speech and look for artifacts of childhood patterns. Does everyone call it a "pop" or is it a "soda"? Did you have a nunney, a binky, or simply a pacifier?

- Observe how you respond to others—do you approach? Retreat? Wait for their direction? Is this a result of parental modeling? Early childhood experiences? Your temperament?

- Do your observations show that you are a good listener? Advice giver? Or a nurturing person?

Observing the Internal You

- Observe and record the various choices you make throughout the week, including choices about what and when to eat, or wear, or where to go? What do these choices say about how and what you value?

- Discover or perhaps re-discover your gifts and your talents. Maybe you are one of the Frisbee catchers, or one who can fetch or roll over. Identify your gifts, your talents, not just the obvious ones, and not just those highlighted in your role at home or at work. Rather, discover those talents revealed in the quiet of your dreams, the solitude of your thoughts, and those spontaneous interactions that are sprinkled throughout your day.

- Do your talents take shape in creative projects, or in organizational skills?

- Do you have an eye for aesthetics, or the nose and taste of a gourmet?

- Are you a dreamer, a doer, a planner, or one who is spontaneous?

As you review your observations did you find that you were re-awakened to the uniqueness of you? Can you now make a commitment to honoring that uniqueness? If so, then read on and let Bud be your guide.

Dog-ma 2:
The Dog-ma of Awakened Hopes and Dreams

I think we are drawn to dogs because they are the uninhibited creatures we might be if we weren't certain we knew better.

—George Bird Evans

I'm not sure if Bud has dreams, goals, or visions of mountains to climb, but he is most certainly less bound by the constraints that often imprison my own dreams. There are times when he is simply gazing out the window and it appears, to me, that while his body remains with me, his spirit is soaring elsewhere.

As you reflect on the image of Bud simply gazing out the window, are you aware of the times this has happened to you? Can you remember times when your body was still but your soul soared to distant places of challenge, wonder, and experience?

Sadly, for many of us, the demands of practicality and the barrage of the requirements of daily life have taken center stage in our lives. With so much of our energy and attention given over to getting through the day, we may have little left to dream. For many of us, the call to be 'realistic' ("come on, get real") has echoed so loudly that the frequency and depth of our dreaming has been diminished and with it, much of life's radiance. How sad.

But this was not always the case, nor need it continue to remain so. There was a time, perhaps it was last week, or last year, or maybe it was well past in your childhood, but there was a time when you were able to attend to all the demands of your daily life and at the same time find time to dream of days and ways to come. Granted, some of that of which we dreamt may now be unrealistic or beyond our reach, but that doesn't mean *all* of our dreams are out of reach. Perhaps your ability to soar has been constricted by your own use of words and thoughts that label your hopes and dreams as "silly," or "impossible," or "that will never happen." Perhaps your hopes and dreams have been dealt the worst of all fates, the fate of "someday."

Over the course of the past 27 years I have seen too many unhappy people holding back and simply waiting for their "someday." You know how that goes: "someday" when I have an extra dollar; "someday" when the kids are grown; "someday" after I retire. Well, why wait

Body at rest—spirit in flight.

for someday? Look around. Someday is NOW! Someday is *this* day. Let your spirit soar. Today is the day to dream, not as escape, but as a process of blazing new trails for your life to follow.

A Bud-ism: Lessons on Hopes and Dreams

The call to dream, to look around the corner, is not to suggest that the present moment is not of importance nor of real consequence. The truth is that the experience of this moment will stimulate you to dream of what may be. You know the concept: some people look at what *is* and ask *why;* others ask *why not.*

As you increase your awareness of *what is,* you will become more aware of that which you want to keep, that which you wish to increase, and that which is missing. It is in this awareness of "what is" that your thoughts of what *could be* become aroused. It is at this moment of life that you can begin to dream of "why not."

So find a spot to simply rest and let go. For a tiny part of this day, a fraction of your life, let go of the "have to's" and "the shoulds." As you let your body rest and your mind become free of demands—allow your spirit to take flight.

The following lessons from Bud are provided not only to help you increase your awareness of your dreams but to assist you in reclaiming them as worthy of pursuit.

Back to the Future

- What happened to your dreams of yesterday? Where did you fashion yourself to be at this stage of your life? What experiences did you dream of having by now?

- Look to see how many of your past dreams have been given life.

- Re-experience the radiance these dreams have given to your life.

- Identify the dreams unfulfilled. Do they still call out for recognition? Or have other dreams... visions... aspirations taken their place?

Flight without Constraint

- Now without worry of resources or responsibilities, what are the dreams—the hopes and images—that move you? Remember dreams need not—should not—be burdened with constraints of how or when. Don't inhibit your dreams with thoughts of "that's silly" or "I could never." Simply dream and become aware of the *you* that the dream portrays.

- Again, without the restrictions of real world concerns, where would your soul take you if you allowed it to take flight? Would it be to new locations, or a different time? Would your destination be to another style of being, or simply to a more developed you? Does it involve different peoples, places, activities, and things?

- If, somehow, when you wake tomorrow you realized that you were the person, in the place, doing the things that are your dreams, what would *you* and what would your *life* look like? Why not write this down! Dreams can come true, but they first have to be retained.

Baby Steps—Dreams to Realities

It is not important that you plan ways to achieve your dreams, at least not at this point. Your task is to nurture your ability to dream. Nurture it as you would any of your other gifts and abilities. You need to structure time to attend to dreaming.

Identify a place where you can free yourself, if only briefly, from the constraints of today so that you can practice dreaming of tomorrow. Your task is simply to dream and be aware of those dreams. Let them once again give radiance to your life.

But there is nothing wrong with taking baby steps toward fulfilling those dreams, so:

- Select one of your dreams.

- Now imagine that you made a series of steps from 1-10 with the fulfillment of the dream resting at the last (10th) step. Where would you place yourself currently? Are you on the ground floor? Or perhaps, you have moved up the stairs and now rest on Stair 3?

- What could you do in the next week, month, year to move one—just one—step closer to the dream? Identify what this is and now, commit to doing it. Do it, even if it is one baby step.

It is with baby steps that spirits take flight.

Dog-ma 3:
The Dog-ma of Richness
of Your World

To a dog, the whole world is a smell.

—Anonymous

I am constantly amazed at Bud. I've watched him on so many occasions as he wakes and greets his day. Unlike his owner, Bud *does not* approach his day with head down, mumbling a perfunctory good morning to those in his path as he stumbles for his coffee. No, Bud wakes with a stretch. It is a stretch that he performs in almost a reverent ritual of preparation. First, he starts with the hind legs, bending his head high, and then he pulls back, stretching out his shoulders, lowering his head as if to limber his neck. It is a process not to be rushed. It is not a mindless routine simply brushing and running... he truly appears to feel each muscle as it awakes.

Having moved his body and his muscles into a ready state, Bud approaches the open door. He moves slowly and deliberately toward the door and takes a few steps into the world. But then he stops. He stops, not with a halt that signals he has forgotten something. No, he stops as if experiencing this world… this backyard… for the first time.

There he is, snout poised high in the air. He gathers in all the world has to offer this morning. He greets the sensation with his full attention and appears to savor each breath as one testing a new wine or food on his palate. What a wonderful experience that must be, experiencing the world for the first time.

Bud has been given a special gift. Actually, all dogs have been given this gift, or perhaps more accurately stated, they have been spared the curse of human nature to have "an almost infinite capacity for taking things for granted" (Aldous Huxley). Bud doesn't take his stretch, or his first experience of the morning air for granted. How lucky to be him!

When was the last time you've taken a deep breath—a really deep breath—and were aware of all the richness in that experience? When was the last time that you were fully aware of the magic to be found in your chest expanding and tightening, your heart faintly beating in the distance, the smell of the spring time or the residue of an afternoon shower in the air. These are diamonds waiting to be mined.

Each day you are afforded the gift of breath and the wonders of exquisite smells. Breath that is so precious that it sustains life, and smells that can invite your memories, stir your feelings and color your moods. Each breath is an opportunity for you to embrace life and with each exhale, to celebrate your being, your very existence. How powerful, how inviting, if only you would pause *to be aware.*

But it is not just the sense of smell and the process of breathing that offer such delights. Perhaps each day you leave your house by foot or car and travel the beaten path to your assigned destination. As you travel you may become lost in the chatter of the radio, the repetitive traffic noise, or even thoughts of evenings past or the anticipated challenges of the day. Perhaps you, like me and so many others, travel to your destination while at the same time missing the wonders of the journey.

Certainly you've seen a sunset and sunrise. You've noticed the neighbors' lovely azalea or flower bed. You even can remember marveling at the resiliency of the willow as it bent in response to the winds of an upcoming storm. You have experienced these riches of our world. But when? How long ago? Have you fallen pray to exer-

Awake to the songs of life.

cising that infinite capacity to take things for granted? If so, then it's time wake up. It's time to respond to the alarm clock with a preparatory stretch, taking time to pause, not because you forgot something, but because you are overwhelmed by the riches this world presents. That's what Bud does.

A Bud-ism: Learning to be Aware of the Richness of the World

Look at him. He sits, snout poised and posed to gather in all the world has to offer. He knows the world is rich and stimulating. It is the same for you. You just need to stop and take it in!

I know this is not new to you, but it helps to be reminded. I can remember talking to a dear friend of mine and 'complaining' about how difficult it was to jog in the morning with Bud. I explained to my friend that we start to run and then he stops and sniffs. Then he takes off and then stops and looks around. Then he takes off again, only to stop and smell something else, or perhaps mark a special spot. Well, as I went on, my friend interrupted me by simply saying, "Maybe you should too." Taken back just a bit, and knowing my friend's somewhat twisted sense of humor I asked, "What do you mean… mark?" "No," he responded. "Simply stop, take time to look and smell and experience the world, rather than simply jog past it." Wow! What a great recommendation. What a good friend. That is maybe what Bud was trying to tell me—but I'm a bit hard headed and may need to hear it twice. Perhaps you are as well?

Stop, Look and Listen

Rather then starting your day on "automatic," get up just a few minutes earlier than usual and pause as you exit your door. Look and listen as if this were your first encounter with the world.

- What do you observe?
- What sounds greet you?
- What appears different since you last took time to notice? Are the trees responding to the changing season? Do the shadows on the building mark the changing positions of our sun? Are the birds preparing for new families, or moving to warmer climates? Is there silence in this morning, or the rhythms of your city, your town waking?

Rather than travel that all too familiar path to work, or school, or running one of the many chores that occupy your time, find a new route. It will force you to pay attention.

- Pay attention to the surroundings and riches of your journey. How does this 'path' differ from the way you usually travel?

The Aroma of Your World

Stop as you enter a room and close your eyes. For just a moment, take in all that you can with one deep breath. Breathe in the life... the presence of that room.

- Perhaps it will be the scent of fresh cut flowers, or coffee brewing in the morning that greets you.

- Perhaps, it will be the aroma of baked goods, or fresh fruit that stimulates your senses.

- Or, perhaps it is the newsprint, or the copy toner, or a co-worker's aftershave or perfume that engulfs you.

In whatever form, this breath and these aromas are gifts that are yours for the taking, if you simply stop and are aware.

Life is a bouquet.

The Gift of Night

Embrace the sights, the sounds, the aroma and feeling of the night. Go outside. Sit quietly. Listen. Take a deep breath. Close your eyes and experience the night as a child on her first camping trip. Feel the coolness, perhaps the dampness of the evening air. Sense the stillness of the world as the day winds down.

Become aware of the sounds, the sights, and the feel of the world of the evening as night begins to awake.

There are so many wonderful experiences to be embraced, if only you could shed your human capacity for taking it all for granted. For the remainder of the week, try focusing on one channel through which you experience the world. Use your eyes to see as if it were the first time. Chew slowly to savor the taste of your evening meal. Find time to touch and be touched.

What wonderful gifts each of these are... and all you have to do is take the time to be aware and accept them!

Dog-ma 4:
The Dog-ma of Life's Simplicities

Dogs are our link to paradise.
They don't know evil or jealousy or discontent.
To sit with a dog on a hillside on a glorious
afternoon is to be back in Eden, where doing
nothing was not boring—it was peace.

—Milan Kundera

What a thought, what an image: "...to sit with a dog on a hillside... it was peace."

Do you remember the days when your life was about sitting on hillsides, rolling down hills, or playing in the rain? There was a time, not so long ago nor in some distant galaxy, that the feel of mud between your toes, a snowflake gently captured on your tongue or eyelashes, or the simple act of running through a sprinkler, were enough to make your day.

For many of us, our mantra of life has become to do more, to achieve more, to acquire more! Yet these activities, these apparently endless pursuits, while adding to an already cluttered life, seem to fail to provide the peace we once found in the simplicities of childhood.

Perhaps you too have become a victim. A victim of work, deadlines, 401K's, mortgage payments, college loans, and solving world problems. Perhaps you have become a victim who now has lost the awareness and the joy of Life's Simplicities. Perhaps your day, like that of so many others, is packed from the moment you awake to the moment you find escape in sleep. Perhaps you find yourself rushing here—rushing there—and failing to find a moment for reflection. Is that the tempo of your world? If so, it is a tempo that has neither time nor place for the process of sitting on a hillside, doing nothing—being at peace. And that is sad.

Certainly life calls us to serious business. We do have responsibilities and real life concerns, which can neither be ignored nor minimized. But just as we can not ignore nor minimize the 'business' of life, we need to guard that we are not absorbed by them, nor magnify them to the point where they become all that we see life offering.

As you watch children indulging in the simple pleasures of life you may begin to remember a time when you, too, knew how to embrace these simple pleasures. Perhaps you are taken by the faint memory of a time

The joy of simple pleasures.

when you, too, ran joyfully down the side of a hill, twirled in the wind, spread the seeds of a dandelion, or watched that tiny ant working so hard to retrieve a piece of food. These are not simply artifacts of yesterday; they are invitations for today.

These memories, as faint as they may be, are 'callings' not to be dismissed. They are beacons through our daze. They are invitations throughout each of our days to embrace, welcome, and enjoy life's simplicities. These memories may bring with them a feeling of want, even a sense of envy and maybe a flight into thoughts of "if only I could."

Well, the truth is, YOU CAN! The opportunity to indulge in life's simple pleasures remains. It didn't go anywhere. Life's joys are still to be found in its simplicities. If only you are aware. Perhaps the lessons from Bud will re-awaken that awareness.

A Bud-ism: Lesson on Engaging Life's Simplicities

"To sit with a dog on a hillside on a glorious after-noon is to be back in Eden..."

Hopefully the image created by these beautiful words brings not just a smile to your lips, but a sigh as well. If so, then embrace that sigh. Embrace it as a sign of your own longing to find Eden, not just on a hillside, or in a glorious afternoon, or the companionship of a dog, but in the simplicity of life that surrounds you.

Take time to reflect, remembering when you engaged in life's simplicities. Then, challenge yourself not only to find your Eden, your place of peace, but to increase your awareness of the joy to be found in all of Life's Simplicities.

Finding your Eden?

Where is it? Or when is it that you feel that sense of joy... that sense of peace?

- Is it in an early morning walk, or the quiet of an evening under the stars?

- Is it in viewing your child, so innocent, lay like an angel fast asleep?

- Is it in marveling at a spider casting her web, or a bird building her nest?

- Is it simply in the moments when you are alone, at the end of your day?

- Will the peace be discovered in the song of the morning birds, the breeze of a summer day, the beauty of newly fallen snow, or the refreshment of a spring rain?

- Is that sense of calm—the gift of peace—to be found in the warmth of a morning shower, or the solitude of an evening bath?

All of these remain... waiting for you.

Joyous Act of Living

Perhaps for you, the joy of life is the simple activities of your youth and childhood. Take some time to remember... to revisit... to recommit.

- Is Eden to be found as you sit on the hillside, or in rolling down a hill?

- Perhaps your joy is to be delivered not only in the spring rain, but in a childlike romp through a sprinkler or by squishing mud through your toes.

- Maybe life's entertainment will be found in watching ants tirelessly maintaining their colony, or a spider weaving its magic, or a butterfly gracefully visiting blooms of varying colors.

No matter how big—or how old—hillsides becken, as does the sprinkler, the mud, and the magic of all life's creatures.

Trying a New Perspective

Radindranath Tagone provides us with the following suggestion: "Do not say, 'It's morning' and dismiss it with a name of yesterday. See it for the first time as a newborn child that has no name."

See it for the first time... Wow, if only we could.

It is not important for us to change our day. We really don't need to try to make something happen. The task is simply to encounter whatever comes our way differently, as if seeing it for the first time. Take this week and try it. Just imagine that you stepped into each day this week as if it were your first... or your last! Really! Take a moment and try to get into the perspective of a person who is new to your daily experiences. Or, if it is easier, imagine that today will be your last opportunity to ever experience all that is presented during the course of this, your typical day. Now...

- How would the shower feel?
- How would the warmth of the sun, or the crispness of the air, be received?

- Would your greeting of 'good morning' have any more meaning? And, would you reflect before responding to the question—'how are you'?

- How might you savor each moment if you accepted it was a moment not to be reclaimed?

There are so many opportunities to embrace, to enjoy, and to find peace in life's simplicities if we only take the time—make the room—and are open to them. Regardless of how long it has been since last you sat, "on a hillside on a glorious afternoon," the truth is the hillside remains, as does the glorious afternoon, all that is missing is *you*.

Section II
Acceptance

Life is 10 percent what you make it,
and 90 percent how you take it.

—Irving Berlin

Bud has a 'cousin' named Gus. Gus is a five-year-old Jack Russell terrier. Needless to say, Gus is a bit energetic, but it is wonderful to watch them together. There is Bud, stretched out enjoying the warmth of an afternoon sun and along comes Gus, prodding, taunting, almost pleading for Bud to play. After a few unsuccessful attempts to ignore the playful pup and with a sense of obligatory 'family duty', Bud will slowly rise, stretch—first the front, then the back legs—and then he sets off on a wild chase. It is amazing—14 years old and yet he still has bursts of speed and agility reflective of his youth. But he is not young. He knows that. His preparatory stretch reveals that awareness and acceptance of his changing body. Further, his rapid return to that comfortable spot in the sun is a clear statement that Bud can relish the joys of aging. Bud is aware of his changes—his needs—his 'self'.

In the previous section you were challenged to look deep. You were asked to take time to look very closely, very deeply at yourself, at others, and even at the world that surrounds you. Hopefully you did. Hopefully, you discovered, or rediscovered, many new things about yourself, those close to you, and the world about you.

But for some of us, looking deeply and becoming aware is like using one of those wonderful makeup mirrors. You know the ones. On one side is a regular mirror but on the other side is a mirror that magnifies everything ten-fold! Looking into that side of the mirror certainly makes you aware.

While at first your gaze may be directed simply to the evenness of your makeup, or to the gentle curve of an eyebrow, or perhaps the length of a side burn, but the magnification shows everything. It highlights each line, wrinkle and discoloration. The characteristics of your face all seem to shout for attention. And for some of us, this awareness is responded to with an 'Ouch'!

But why should you respond to the sight of your wrinkles, your lines, your moles or even your warts with an ouch? This is you. This is how you look. This is how "You" are at this point in time. That's not an ouch… it's YOU!

Now that you have increased your awareness of what *is,* it is time to increase your *acceptance* of all that is! Such acceptance, as you will see, does not mean whole-sale approval. It does not mean you need to roll over and simply surrender. No, change is allowed. But even for those things you wish to change, the first step is to accept and embrace that which is. Remember, *"…life is 90 percent how you take it."*

So your choice is simple. You can lament the fact that you no longer have the energy nor the agility to race about as you once did. Or, you can *accept* the truth that you *can* be playful for a brief time and then relish the enjoyment of stretching out in the warmth of the sun. That's acceptance and it can be great. Just ask Bud!

The lessons to follow will help guide your acceptance of what is, and in so doing, help you to see the value in what is, which will all help create what will soon be.

Dogma 5:
This is ME!

If one is a greyhound, why try
to look like a Pekingese?
—Dame Edith Sitwell

A greyhound, so sleek, graceful, and proud, with strides so smooth and long. How sad it would be to imagine that deep behind those soulful eyes was a desire to be anything but that lovely animal. So sad if days were spent wishing for shorter legs, curlier hair, a prancing gate, or a ribbon in the hair. If one is a greyhound, why try to look like anything else? Indeed!

Perhaps, like me, you emerged from your journey into awareness with a clearer view of grey hair, where once was only blonde; or perhaps no hair, where once there was some? Maybe you've noticed the muscles that once were well defined now appear to be on vacation or in permanent retirement. Or maybe your discovery was that the smoothness of skin that once greeted you in the morning mirror has been replaced by lines, some valleys and a texture and color that is now uneven and somewhat blotchy. Yep, becoming aware can be like gazing into one of those magnifying mirrors. But the truth be told, this is you. This is the you that needs to be accepted, the you that needs to be embraced. This is the you that truly deserves that acceptance.

Acceptance of *me*—especially the changing me—can be difficult, if the spectrum of our focus is only on our changing bodies and body image. Living at a time and in a culture where images of youth and beauty abound and actually invade our senses, it is understandable how one can begin to view his or her own changing body as something less than 'ideal' and maybe even something as less than acceptable, even negative. But negative? Negative when compared to what? To whom? Pictures in a magazine? Personalities on television or in movies?

The failure to accept our own self in all its beauty needs to be confronted. The beauty of you is exactly that. It is beautiful because it is you.

I remember listening to a college commencement speaker. She was an 83-year-old Sister of the Order of St. Francis. Prior to her comments to the graduates, she thanked her gracious hosts for their hospitality and then reflected on a recurring experience that she found quite curious. She noted that many people she met seemed to

Simply Bud—perfectly content being himself.

be somewhat obsessed with age. They would ask, "Sister, how old are you?" and then, she continued, "When I would tell them I was 83, they would say, but you don't look 83!"

As I sat there listening, I found myself agreeing with all of those who preceded me, she didn't look 83! But before I got too far in my own reflections, she interrupted my thoughts by concluding: "...but this is how 83 looks on me."

What a wonderful thought. This is how 28... 35.... 45... or 83 looks on *me*. It is my look—my style—the evidence of my years of life's experience, and that is something to embrace. That is something to be celebrated!

Accepting "ME" demands that you embrace the total package:

- not just age spots, but the rich memories that come with them;
- a changed body, as well as a changed and changing perspective;
- the reality of less energy, as well as increased wisdom, and;
- the appearance of limitations along with new capabilities.

The Bud-isms to follow will hopefully assist you in both your recognition of this reality and your acceptance of it.

A Bud-ism: Lessons on Accepting ME

Bud has been told that he really doesn't look like a dog of 14 years (that's 91 for you and me). But if he could talk I am sure he would say "thank you," and then add "but this is how 14 looks on me!"

He's grayer now, and he takes a bit more time to get the body moving, and clearly he naps more than before. But even when surrounded by the more energetic, smoother coated, quicker reflexed 'cousins', he doesn't attempt to hide nor apologize. He simply embraces that this is how beauty, speed, agility, grace... look now. This is Bud!

What a lesson to learn. Learning to accept your uniqueness, your style, your *self,* is the focus of this Bud-ism. So take a deeper look at, and reflection of those many changes that have occurred over the course of your life. Identify them, name them, accept them, and then celebrate them, because they are *you.*

Body and All

- While your hair may have changed its color, a closer inspection will reveal the beauty of its multi-colors. How vibrant!

- The outline of the abdomen, where once was a 'six-pack', may now give evidence of the creation and nurturance of life. What a blessing!

Thoughts, Feelings, Style and More

- Perhaps, like Bud, it takes a little more time to get the body moving—and the reflexes are not as sharp as in days gone by, but with this change you may have also cultivated your ability to sit and reflect on all that is really important. How enriching!

- Perhaps you find that you are more aware of your feelings and freer to express them. What a gift!

- No longer burdened with adolescent concerns about the opinions of others, maybe now you can sing a tiny bit louder at the office party or church, or wear those pants that feel so comfortable. How freeing!

- The dreams of being a professional athlete or Olympic medalist may have faded, now in their place is a backyard catch with your 'little leaguer' or the sideline encouragement of your future Olympian. How rewarding!

- And maybe your old in-line skates don't move as smoothly as they once did, or the kite needs more wind power to compensate for the loss of foot speed, and maybe you now get 'looks' where once you had an audience… but regardless, the truth is you still can do the things you loved. How wonderful!

As you continue your journey into awareness, you will come to accept that nothing is really lost, just exchanged. You would make a very bad nine-year-old, or teen, or …? You make a great *you*. So smile. Say to yourself, 'Thank you'. Thank you, for this is how I look on me.

If you do, perhaps then you will celebrate the fact that you are a Greyhound, or a Pekingese, and not wistfully desire to be the other.

Dog-ma 6:
Me as Less than Perfect

To err is human—to forgive, canine.

—Anonymous

I can remember entering the kitchen that morning, a little tired from the night before, a tiny bit of a headache (again from the night before), and now being greeted by the remnants of the night before! The bones of chicken wings, remains of appetizers, even tiny pieces of crust from the pies were strewn from trash to culprit! There he lay, as innocent as could be, belly distended, deep in sleep, seemingly without a care in the world. BAD DOG! (Well, not really... but he could at least *look* guilty.)

As you can imagine, regardless of how cute the Bud-dog appeared, it was time to wake this sleeping prince. He was in the DOG HOUSE! And besides, I was concerned that some of the things he ate may not be very good for him. Oh, and yes, he really needed to BE TAUGHT a lesson! You know, his nose would be taken to the scraps, my finger firmly shaken, and in my best authoritative voice, I would proclaim, "NO! BAD!"

That's it... just "no" and "bad" but not "bad dog."

He really isn't a bad dog, he's just a DOG! Bud simply was doing what seemed to be a good thing at the time. So while he may lower his head and give me the 'please forgive me, I'm so cute look', he really doesn't feel guilty, and that's because he's not human. Lucky Dog!

Humans are certainly unique. We make mistakes and then we have this wonderful capacity for beating ourselves up forever for these mistakes. Guilt—a characteristic of the human condition. How un-dog like.

Perhaps at this point you are saying to yourself, "Yeah? And your point is?" Doesn't it make sense that when you screw up you should feel guilty?

Let me ask you to take a moment and really stop and think before responding to the following question. Ready? Have you ever *chosen* to screw up? Have you ever chosen to make a mistake? I can imagine that your almost automatic response is to say "Of course." But did you really? Did you really *choose* to screw up? I'm not suggesting that you didn't foul up the works or somehow make a mistake, maybe even a huge one, but was that what you chose to do?

Less than perfect... but not guilty about it.

I bet on closer inspection you will see that at any one time you chose to act in ways that seem, at least at that moment, to be the best choice available. It only becomes a mistake later, after you have time to review your choices from a different perspective.

Humans have the wonderful ability to think, "If only I had known." We make great Monday morning quarterbacks and back seat drivers. You know the maxim, hindsight is 20/20! But hindsight is a silly exercise if we only use it to make ourselves feel shameful and guilt ridden over our decisions. Decisions that we made *without* the benefit of such hindsight! The truth of the matter is that we make the best decisions we can with the information and conditions present at that moment. There is no hindsight or better options apparent. Then, why feel guilty over doing the best we could at that moment?

So, do we really select mistakes? Not really. Are our decisions sometimes viewed by ourselves and others as mistakes? Absolutely. That will never change; that's being fallible. That's being human.

I know it can be an inconvenience, but our fallibility is a fact. So, let's accept it and move on.

Now please don't get me wrong. I am not suggesting that we shouldn't learn from these experiences. I am not suggesting we shouldn't "vow" not to repeat them. What I'm suggesting is that learning from past "mistakes" and committing to make different choices in the future can occur and probably will occur more effectively without the additional needless guilt that we place upon ourselves. Time spent in the "dog house" is useful only to the degree that we reflect upon our choices, understand the conditions that led to our selections, and attempt to develop alternative responses should we find ourselves in the same position in the future. To be placed in and remain in the "dog house" beyond this point is simply counterproductive.

Bad dog? Not really. Just a dog, doing a dog thing. He may pay the price of his action throughout the day (I'm not sure if that pepper shooter is going to sit well?) and he may even learn from this experience (and begin to think twice before indiscriminately attacking the trash). But at least he won't need help with resolving his shame and guilt.

Ah, to be a dog. Perhaps there are lessons to be learned?

A Bud-ism: Lessons on Acceptance of a "Less than Perfect" Me

You know, Bud was moving really slowly that day. I think the peppers were a bit too much.

Thankfully, he'll survive and will most certainly party another day. But maybe, just maybe, this day of discomfort will help him to become a more discerning trash picker, or a non-trash picker.

But the lesson I learned that day, watching my poor old 'partied-out' Bud, wasn't to be discerning in what I eat (something I still need to learn), but to move on to the next moment, and leave the sack cloth and ashes behind.

After I woke him and pointed out the errors of his way, he did provide me the obligatory, ear down, sad look. But it was short lived. He moved on. He came to me to have his head rubbed. He barked at the cat. He stretched out in the sun. In other words, he went on with his life. He continued on without a single incident of shame or guilt-motivated retreat.

Mistakes happen. Decisions that seemed right can be re-evaluated and re-identified as poor only after the fact. We can and perhaps would be wiser to learn from them. But learning from our mistakes doesn't require us to feel bad about our *self.* In fact, such feelings of shame and guilt can actually interfere with our ability to learn. So accepting the less-than-perfect me may be achieved if we practice the following.

The Fact of Fallibility

- Practice accepting the fact of your fallibility. Perhaps you have made a mistake. Maybe someone noticed that you made an error in the family check book, or you made a wrong turn, or perhaps you misunderstood an appointment time. So? Accept it. Accept it as a mistake, not as a horrible thing to be denied or defended, but just as evidence of your humanity.

- Practice saying, "I'm sorry." Say you're sorry for the inconvenience that your decision or your action may have caused another, but *not* sorry for being a person who made that decision. If knowing what you know now would have altered your decision, then why should you apologize for not previously having had this knowledge?

Accepting Self and Others as Fallible

- Imagine that your friend approached you, very upset about the "terrible mistake" she had made. As she shares her story, regardless of the details, would you feel that she was a terrible person? Would you believe that she should feel horrible, guilty now and well into the future for her mistake? Or, would you be able to recognize that while the consequence of what she did may be pretty serious, she simply made a mistake. She made a faulty decision, but one that was the best she could have made *at that time.*

- Take a moment to review one of your "major" mistakes. Perhaps it would help to actually write it down. Now treat yourself as you would treat your friend. Try to step out of the role of mistake maker and simply be the caring, listening friend.

- Review the elements and conditions that existed at the time of your mistake. Were you tired, upset, under pressure? Was there something happening that was interfering with your clear vision of all available choices and their likely outcomes? Is there any real benefit to feeling guilty or shameful, either now or long into the future about this event?

- And lastly, if there is something that you have been feeling a little guilty about, or maybe even a tad worried that it may be discovered, go now and announce it. Tell someone. Announce it, not as a statement of pride, nor as one of shame, and not as a confession or to seek forgiveness. Announce it simply as an event in your life that you may, or may not, need help rectifying. No shame... just acceptance of a less than perfect me!

Dog-ma 7:
The World As Is...

My dog is usually pleased with what I do,
because she is not infected with the concept
of what I "should" be doing.

—Lonzo Idolswine

Dogs are certainly the most accepting of creatures. They tolerate our mood swings, they are willing to wait as we make last minute adjustments and corrections to our plans for a walk, and they even humor us as we dress them in booties, sweaters, and an endless variety of bows and ribbons. Dogs are accepting because they appear to take what is... as it *is*, rather than *demand* that it be different.

Unlike most humans, dogs simply respond to the "what is" of the moment and free themselves from the "shoulds," "musts" and "have to's" that typically guide most of our days. This human capacity to turn what may be a "good idea" or a "desirable condition" into an absolute *should* or *must*, can certainly lead to many problems.

Imagine that you actually believed that your dog *had* to wear a sweater, booties, or some other such apparel before leaving the house for his morning constitution? Now don't get me wrong; I'm not suggesting that placing protective clothing on some dogs is wrong. Some dogs may actually enjoy the added warmth of a doggie-sweater. But imagine that you actually took a good idea, like trying to insulate the dog from the cold, and turned it into a absolute must: DOGS MUST WEAR SWEATERS! Just think of it. If you believed this truly was an absolute must, like the 11th commandment, then you would be riddled with guilt and anxiety each time you failed to do this. Further, you would most likely become infuriated, enraged if someone else abused their pooch by ignoring this dictum.

While I am sure you agree that such an absolute, obligatory approach to dog garments would be extreme, what you may not realize is that you, like me, live in a tapestry of *shoulds, musts,* and *have to's.* The pressures of living such a life of "obligation" often takes form in our feelings of anxiety, guilt, and anger.

You may hold a number of beliefs that started out as simply good and desirable ideas but which have turned

Accepting the world as it is and taking it all as it comes.

into your own set of absolute laws about the way the world is supposed to be. If this happens you can expect to find yourself being extremely upset whenever one of these laws is violated. For example, have you ever been rushing to an important meeting only to find yourself stuck in highway traffic? Now, it is a good idea, a desirable idea, to get to your meeting on time. Missing the appointment or being late can result in consequences which are not desirable, and it is a good idea to avoid these consequences if possible. But take a look at your reactions. Do they reflect the perspective that the traffic jam is just an inconvenience? Do they reflect a perspective of disappointment? Do they fit the moment? Hopefully so. But for some of us, a situation like a traffic jam elicits rising blood pressure, squirming bodies, and blaring car horns. Not very productive? Not even necessary.

Perhaps you have found yourself becoming angry—really angry—at the way another person is acting. You know, the guy in front of you who is not moving even though the light has turned green? Or, your teenager *never* takes out the garbage as he is *supposed to!*

Why the reaction? How is it that if good ideas and desirable conditions are not met, the situation somehow is elevated to the point that it starts to feel like a major catastrophe?

Our experiences, whether being stuck in traffic, stood up for a date, or confronted by mounds of trash, are actually comprised of two separate elements. First, in each of these encounters there is some real world event: there is a line of traffic; I am waiting at the restaurant by myself; I see the trash can filled to the top. But in addition to these real world events, I am also perceiving and giving meaning to the events. And this is the culprit!

What we tell ourselves about the meaning of an event is the source of these emotional reactions. If you voiced what was going on inside your head at the moment you were stuck in traffic, running late for an important meeting, would you say: "Darn, this is a problem. These things happen. This is going to cause some real inconvenience. I may lose the account or have to reschedule this meeting. I'll have to call and let them know I'm not going to be there"? Or, is your outrage and panic more likely expressed in reaction to your believing: "This is unfair. This can't be happening. I can't stand this! I *have to* be on time. This is a horrible, unbearable, catastrophic situation!"

The truth be told, if this was a horrible, unbearable, catastrophic injustice your reactions may make some sense. But it's not. Is it really horrible? Is it unbearable, or isn't it up to you how you will bear it? Is it a catastrophe, or a problem?

If you experience life this way, as a series of *musts* and *have to's,* then anytime those "musts" are not met you will probably experience these situations as unbearable, horrible, and catastrophic. You will believe you really "can't stand" these events and you will react with panic or anger. If, instead, you see problems and mistakes as inconveniences and challenges to work through, then lack of fulfillment simply results in disappointment, not disaster. With this perspective, the traffic jam is just an inconvenience perhaps significant to you, but not unbearable. Viewing life this way will not raise your blood pressure or cause headaches or engender road rage (all of which do little for moving traffic but a lot to compound your problems). Keeping a perspective about problems will stimulate you to use your energy to problem solve, which is certainly a lot more desirable.

Changing your perspective requires that you surrender the belief that you can define the way the world is *sup-*

posed to be, and replace it with an acceptance of the way the world *is*.

This is not a glass half-full perspective. No, what is being suggested is that we accurately identify our reality, with its ups and downs, and then celebrate that which deserves celebrating and attempt to navigate through that which does not. As the cartoon/philospher Ziggy reminds us, "You can complain because the roses have thorns, or you can rejoice because thorns have roses." To which I would add, that in seeing both, you will be able to enjoy the flower while minimizing the pricks of the thorns.

A Bud-ism: Lessons on Accepting the World as It Is

Bud can be a finicky eater. On more than one occasion I've seen him approach the bowl, give it a hard look, sniff, and then look at me as if to say "Really?"

What I have never encountered in these situations is an enraged dog. No, he sniffs at the bowl and then after a brief protest, either eats what is there or waits until later. Bud can distinguish between food that he finds less than desirable and food that he "can't stand." He accepts "what is" for what it *is*—nothing worse—and he attempts to make the best of it. This is your lesson. To accept what is and make the best of it.

Recognizing the Power of Thoughts

Keeping a "thought" journal is a good idea.

1. When you are upset, truly distraught about something that you are encountering in the day that is not the way you feel it is supposed to be, write it down. Perhaps it is being stuck in traffic, or missing an important meeting, or having to change your plans because of the weather, or having a special meal ruined. Whatever it is, write it down. First describe the event. Be a careful observer. Write down the actual events of the day.

2. Later, re-read or simply reflect on the thing that was so upsetting. Can you hear that voice going off in your head? Write down what you are saying to yourself about the event.

3. Now, take a moment to look at your reactions—your feelings and actions. Do they really seem to make sense in light of the actual event? Or do they only make sense once you take notice of how you have interpreted the event?

Taking Life As It Is

As your journal writing will show, life doesn't always go the way we wish. That is disappointing and it can be truly inconveniencing. But it is as it is—until we try to resolve it. In the meantime, taking life as it *is*—only that bad and no worse—may prove less upsetting.

- Catch your breath, read what you wrote, and ask yourself the following: "Is this a situation that I *really* can't stand, or is it merely undesirable, something I wish didn't happen?" Remember that you in fact are standing it—but you may be standing it *poorly!*

- Replace and "I can't stand it" thinking with: "This is not the way I wanted things to go. It is inconvenient and disappointing, but not a catastrophe. What could I do at this moment to make the situation more productive and more enjoyable, even if only by a little bit?"

You are accepting the event as is, and not making it bigger, worse or more damaging than it really is. If this were the way you saw the event, how would you feel? How would you act?

Practicing

We know that life has butterflies *and* caterpillars, and roses have thorns as well as flowers. We also know that only seeing the caterpillars and the thorns would distort reality and would not lead to happy, productive lives. Similarly, only seeing the flowers and the butterflies equally distorts reality. So the answer? See the world as it *is*—no better, no worse—which will certainly help you navigate it or begin to take steps to make it the way you wish it could be. Seeing the world as it *is*—no better, no worse—is the focus of the following exercise.

Place yourself in the situation listed in Column A and begin to see how changing your thinking from that presented in column B, to that presented in Column C, is both more realistic and more effective for accepting the world as it is. Now try it yourself.

A (The event)	B (One view)	C (A second, considered view)
1. Having a picnic	It's raining & our picnic is ruined. I can't believe this after all the work.	It's raining... darn, let's move and do the picnic indoors.
2. Asking a friend to help you move	It's so unfair he won't help me. Nobody cares about my needs.	It's a disappointment that he doesn't want to help. I'm going to have to get a hand truck or maybe I could find someone else.
3. A person cutting in front of you at the check-out counter	He can't do that. He's horrible. I'll show him!	I would prefer that he didn't do that. I'll ask him if he saw me in line first? I am wondering what's his hurry?

Section III
Authenticity

Money will buy you a pretty good dog, but it won't buy the wag of its tail.

—Henry Wheeler Shaw

No, money won't buy the wag of a dog's tail, because as Martin Buxbaum so aptly stated it, "A dog wags its tail with its heart." And you can't buy that!

With a four footed companion, what you see is what you get. The joyful wag of the tail is simply the outer reflection of the joy in the heart. No deceit, no artificiality... simple authenticity. This is not always true for us, non-dogs.

Your journey into increased awareness may have challenged you to accept all, not just some, of the discoveries of that journey. Now you are summoned to be real—to be true—to be authentic to these discoveries of self and the world.

Being authentic and living authentic lives is not an easy task. We are the products of a time and culture that extolls the value of "image": "It's not *who* you are, but *what* you wear", "It isn't *what* you know, but *who* you know"; and so on. It's all about the surface. You know... perception is reality!

So many of us have fallen trap to this pursuit of the "right way to be" or the "right image to project" that we have forgotten or abandoned the "how we really are." We seem surrounded by implants, Botox, steroid-produced muscles, exaggerated life styles, all pulling us away from what is genuine.

Hopefully your journey into awareness and acceptance has been a profitable venture. Hopefully, you have re-discovered the gift which is you and the wonderful joys to be discovered in the simplicity of the world around us. With this perspective in place, the hyped images inviting you to be "more than you can be," will now fall on your deaf ears. Knowing and accepting yourself places you in a position in which anything less than authentic, less than real, less than true, is less than acceptable.

The lessons to be found in this section will invite you to continue your journey, ever growing in your ability to be Real, Vulnerable and Faithful!

Dogma 8:
Being Real

Recollect that the Almighty, who gave the dog
to be companion of our pleasures and our
toils, hath invested him with a nature
noble and incapable of deceit.

—Sir Walter Scott

Incapable of deceit! Incapable of being a fraud! Incapable of being less than *real!* These are all descriptions of our four footed companions and beacons for our own health and wholeness.

But, to be *real* requires that we shed our masks. It requires us to rid ourselves of all games and lose all the scripts that may have guided us in the past.

Contrary to what Shakespeare suggested, the world is not a stage, nor is your life a play and you an actor in it. No, the world is a gift and your life is a journey to experience. Through it all, it is only when you are willing to be you—and allow others to be as they are—that you will experience the gift of life.

Being real is the process by which you become aware,

accept, and as we will see in the next section, celebrate our authenticity.

There were times, especially early in my career as a psychologist, that I sometimes felt as if I had to put on my "game face" when I would meet a new client. In my eagerness to do it correctly, I would sometimes try too hard and become somewhat artificial in my care and concern.

Often our desire to *do it correctly* or *to be liked* by another forces us to play out a role. We may feel like we are bound to perform or enact certain types of behaviors, such as those associated with being male or female, being a parent, a teacher, or even a psychologist. When we act from a prescribed role, we fail to be real.

To be real requires us to be role-free. To be real requires that we are open, as opposed to defensive, and genuine, as opposed to phony. To be real means at any one time we are congruent, with our words, actions, tones, thoughts, and feelings; we are in concert and expressing a consistent message. Being real, being congruent, means that what we project to the world reflects that which is truly within. There are no hidden agendas or ulterior motives, nor will you find any guises or attempts at deceit. What you see is what is! The tail is wagging only because the heart is, and not in an attempt to win favor.

Just being real... Just being a dog.

So, how does one become real? How are we to shed the masks, the artificial roles, the phoniness? Hopefully you have already discovered a major portion of the answer to these questions.

By becoming more aware and by accepting that awareness, you have hopefully come to appreciate that those discovered realities are far better than any mask or artificial role and script you may have created in the past. Being you is better than any part you could play. Accepting yourself, accepting others, and accepting the world as it is, is better than any game with its illusions and artificiality.

So hopefully your trip through awareness and acceptance have moved you to be *real*. But in addition to awareness and acceptance, there is another ingredient that is essential to becoming real—love. You must become a lover of self, of others, and of life.

In 1927, Margery Williams wrote a beautiful story of love, "The Velveteen Rabbit." In that story readers are introduced to the wisdom of the Skin Horse. In one very poignant section of the story, the horse patiently explains to the rabbit that "Real isn't how you are made. It's a thing that happens to you. When a child loves you for a long, long time, not just to play with, but *really* loves you, then you become *real*."

The Skin Horse tells us this is not an easy nor rapid process, this thing of becoming real. "Generally, by the time you are *real,* most of your hair has been loved off, and your eyes drop out and you get loose in the joints and very shabby. But these things don't matter at all, because once your are *real,* you can't be ugly except to people who don't understand."

To be Real in this way requires that you remove the mask, step out of the role, and allow your actions to be guided by the moment, not by the pre-conceived script of how life is supposed to be. To be real requires that you listen to your inner directions and trust yourself. Trust that you—the real you—is more than good enough. Trust the real you as a person of value, a person of distinction, a person who can not and should not be hidden under a mask, nor limited to one role in a pre-conceived life script. Trust that to be real means that you can't be ugly except to people who don't understand.

A Bud-ism: Learning to Be REAL

Watching the old Budster, even for an hour, is all the instruction one needs on being real. Look at him. At times, he walks slowly as if regally inspecting each subject in his kingdom. Very proper, very controlled—very befitting his royalty. Yet at other times, he bounds out running here, there, back again, aimlessly sprinting, playfully jumping and tugging at his leash. A pup with abandon. These actions are not performed on command. They are not predictable in terms of calendar or hour, nor occasion of the walk. Nor are they inhibited by concerns over appropriateness, or of what others may think. They are simply variations in Bud's style which he acts upon when the spirit moves him.

What you see with Bud is what you get. His actions are not because he is playing a role of "older pup" or in line with a script for "walking with the Master." No! His actions reflect his response to the moment. When his tail wags, or he jumps with abandon, or sits quietly as if in a moment of reflection, he is merely manifesting the directive of his heart—a directive experienced at that moment. He is simply being *real*.

What an image, what a lesson—a lesson to be learned! A lesson that you can learned if you practice the following.

Role-Bound or Role Free?

Have you ever responded to someone's question, "How are you doing?" with a simple "Fine"? How often has that response been given, when the truth was that you were anything but "fine" at the moment? This is not to suggest that you need always to provide accurate, in depth information about yourself. But you are being asked to consider how often your use of expected responses interferes with your genuineness, your REALness?

Consider your role as a male or a female. Have you experienced thoughts, feelings, even actions that have been inhibited or denied because they didn't fit your gender role and you chose to play the role of "male" or "female" rather than being true to your self? What other roles have you adopted? Adult? Child? Teacher? Father? Mother? Sister? Or how about roles such as: "tension reducer," "problem solver," "nice guy," "good/girl," "conservative," "controlling," and the list goes on.

Your task is to identify the various roles you play through the day—and consider the degree to which these roles are true reflections of who you are or simply masks that have inhibited you from being *you*.

Transparency Log

Do you find yourself often saying one thing but actually feeling or thinking something else? If your exterior were transparent, would people see something different inside then what is being projected outside?

Your task is to keep a transparency log. Take a few days to simply write down specific thoughts or feelings you have difficulty expressing. The ones that typically come out in a "disguised" form.

Are there aspects of your self that you keep guarded, maybe even hidden? List them. Identify the conditions in which you feel it necessary to hide these aspects or disguise these thoughts and feelings. Then challenge yourself. Is it really necessary for you to hide these thoughts and feelings? Has it become such a pattern to hide this side of you that you do it without thinking and when not even necessary? If so, then go out and show yourself to the world (or at least a chosen segment of your world) and smile!

Building REAL Connections

In order to grow in a relationship with another, information that you keep private must be moved into the public arena. (It must be made public in that it becomes known by both you and the other.) For *real* connections to occur, not only do you need to make public more of yourself to this other, but you must also be receptive to the feedback the other person may provide.

As you journey toward REAL—share your self with a loved one. Identify some private thought or feeling, some aspect of you that you have kept from another, but now wish to share. Disclose this information as evidence of your desire for a deeper relationship. Allow this special other to more fully know the *real* you. You'll be surprised and delighted with the loving response you will receive since, as the Skin Horse reminds us, "...once you are REAL, you can't be ugly except to people who don't understand."

Dog-ma 9:
Being Vulnerable

A dog wags its tail with its heart.
—Martin Buxbaum

Bud enjoys being rubbed. He especially seems to enjoy being touched on his belly. I'll sometimes watch as he lays down near my feet and gradually maneuvers just so his back is on the floor, his belly straight up, and he presents himself with a look that seems to say: "Ah, come on... just a little." Bud so enjoys being rubbed, and the truth be told, I so much enjoy petting him.

But this is more than a lesson on sensuality and touch. In order for Bud to enjoy the experience of being petted, he needs to be willing to risk having his underbelly exposed. He is vulnerable. Lying on his back would make it difficult for him to escape should he be attacked. Yet somehow he knows that for him to experience the touch he wants, he must risk being attacked or being hurt. He must risk being vulnerable.

If Martin Buxbaum is correct and dogs do wag their

tails with their hearts, then their willingness to be vulnerable extends well beyond their ability to expose their underbellies. They are also willing to share—to expose—their hearts and their feelings.

Risky? Just Consider It!

How risky is it for you to approach another and without any real assurance of acceptance or affirmation, share your feelings? How risky is it to truly wag that tail, when it reveals what is inside, rather than attempt to be coy?

Sadly, the fear of being vulnerable, being unprotected and open to possible hurt, leads many of us to clothe ourselves in protective armor. Now this is not to suggest we should become defenseless. Our four-legged friends know the difference between vulnerability as an opportunity to love as opposed to when it is simply a silly risky invitation to pain.

No, vulnerability without discernment can be dangerous. But defensiveness without discernment can be life robbing. When our defensive posture becomes an armor so impenetrable that it not only keeps hurt out, but also the joy of having our belly rubbed by one who

Vulnerability as a gift of love.

loves us, then it is no longer healthy. Yes, to love and be loved requires that we risk disappointment, rejection, hurt. But perhaps the truth to be learned is, "To love, and to be hurt often, and to love again—that is the brave and happy life." (J.E. Buchrose).

To be real and to move away from the comfort of our artificial scripts, masks and disguises, is risky business. Being real exposes you. It makes you vulnerable to the pain of rejection.

Do you remember the scene in the *Wizard of OZ*, when Dorothy and friends stepped behind the great curtain to see the real wizard. The expression of terror, the sense of panic, the frantic attempt to regain his "image," was painful to watch. Yet it was only through this demasking that this very isolated and lonely man was able to encounter real interactions with real love (as opposed to fear and false adulation to the man on the screen). Terror, yes. But only because he was unsure of the acceptance that was to follow.

Vulnerability opens us to discovery. Risking vulnerability invites you to unmask, and if you are unsure of what is to follow, this invitation may elicit the same sense of panic and the same frantic attempt to regain your "image," exhibited by our grand wizard. But you need to believe that vulnerability also opens you to the experience of real love, and while it takes some braveness to be loving in this way, it is that which results in a happy life.

So it is time to review your use of your protective coats. Time to risk the experience of vulnerability and time to come to know and experience the joy that it can elicit. It is time to roll over—expose your underbelly to those you love—and experience the joy of a loving touch, a real connection.

A Bud-ism: Lessons on Being Vulnerable

When he has to, Bud—this 14-year-old, SPCA special— can look and sound ferocious. But he's not. Thankfully the neighbors' cat and unwanted door-to-door sales people don't know that. Bud doesn't automatically bare his underbelly. He doesn't indiscriminately show his real, vulnerable self to all he encounters. No, for Bud, vulnerability is something he shares as his gift of love. It is his invitation to share and experience together.

When was the last time you dropped your mask, your facade, your defenses and let another experience the real you, the you of that moment? Has it been some time? Was it during a time of crisis, when you were overwhelmed and unable to maintain the shield? Or, have you used your ability to become vulnerable both as a gift to another and an invitation to share, to experience you more deeply? It is this ability that we invite you to develop.

Time to Say Thank You

Take some time to reflect on the special value another has in your life. Perhaps it is your parents, a significant other, a child or children, or a special friend. Really reflect on what he or she means to you and to your life. Now tell them. Write them a good old fashioned letter. Not an email, or a voice mail, or a Hallmark card. No. With pen and paper, in your best script, share with them the joy they bring you. Tell them the needs within you that they meet. Express how important and how valuable they are in your life.

And yes, it is a risk. Telling another all of this certainly gives them power. But it is a power to love you more, so why be afraid?

Time to Step From Behind the Curtain

Unlike our grand wizard, don't wait to be discovered hiding behind that curtain or that mask. Don't wait, isolated and alone, presenting to the world an artificial image. Stop waiting for a Dorothy to find you and free you from your isolation.

Begin to share you. Share your ideas, even if they are not completely complimentary or in agreement to anothers. Share your interests, especially those that you have held secret for too long. Share your dreams, even those that on first blush appear to be only found in Oz.

Share these dreams and this you as a gift to those special others in your life. Share this unprotected you as an invitation to these special people to come to know you, to experience you, and to love you more fully.

Time to Bare Your Underbelly

To rest, undefended physically or emotionally, in the presence of another is risky. However, not to rest in this fashion denies you the opportunity to experience the caring touch, both physically and emotionally, of another, and that denial is life deadening.

Find that person or persons with whom you seek to develop increased intimacy, increased realness, and bare your underbelly. Tell them what you want. Tell them what you wish to experience in your relationship and then ask them if they would respond in the way you desire.

It could be something as small as asking for help with a particular task, or the intimacy of a back rub. Be open, not only to letting the other see into you, but being touched by this other. Your vulnerability is a gift that will touch them deeply. It is only natural that they in turn will want to share their self as well. And, with that sharing, you and yours will grow.

Dog-ma 10:
Being Faithful—Fidelity

*The one absolutely unselfish friend that man
can have in this selfish world, the one that
never deserts him, the one that never proves
ungrateful or treacherous, is his dog.*

—George Graham Vest

It continues to amaze me (and quite often in some ways it humbles me) to realize that regardless of how my day has been, the one consistency to that day will be Bud's greeting and acceptance of me in his life. It may have been a morning that I dashed from the house without even the slightest recognition of his presence, or one in which I stormed through the door to make that one last important phone call. No matter... he'll wait. He'll wait by the door to eagerly greet my return, or if need be, he'll wait outside my office door until the phone call is made. Yes, Bud will wait, not so much because he needs me, but because I need him.

Konrad Lorenz noted that the "fidelity of a dog is a precious gift." For me, it has not only been a precious gift but a valuable life lesson.

I recently had occasion to take my VCR in to get it repaired. The technician looked at the make and model and said "Mister, if I were you I'd toss this one and get a new one. It would be a lot easier and a lot less money." Toss it? I guess that could be the mantra for much of the 21st century.

We have become a disposable society. If it is broke, toss it. If it is simply out of style—too big, or the wrong color—replace it. If it is the one everyone has, then get it too, even if we have two others! And if it will take some work to maintain or develop, then why bother? Just get something—or someone else—that is easier.

This fickle, non-committed approach to life is sadly not restricted to our dealings with things. Pets given as gifts at Christmas all too often become the property of the streets by March. Public promises made to constituents or to stock holders last only as long as they serve the speaker. Vows exchanged at altars, or 'life' commitments made in private, often have less shelf life than the cake used in the celebration.

Sadly, we are becoming a society of the non-committed, the non-faithful. All too often the only fidelity we exhibit is to the moment and to our pleasures. In a society that champions dispose-ability, the fidelity

Faithful and true.

exhibited by our four legged friends may be more than a precious gift, it may be our saving grace, an invaluable life lesson.

> *He is your friend, your partner, your defender, your dog. You are his life, his love, his leader. He will be yours, faithful and true, to the last beat of his heart. You owe it to him to be worthy of such devotion.*
> (Author unknown)

You owe it to him, to those you love, and to yourself to be more like him, faithful to your own true self, and to those you love.

A Bud-ism: Lessons on Fidelity

To be loyal to your best convictions and faithful to that which you value—now, that is a direction for life. To be true and faithful to self and the ideals you hold precious can be quite a challenge:

> *No more important duty can be urged upon those who are entering the great theater of life than simple loyalty to their best convictions.*
> (Edwin Hubbel Chapin)

Loyalty and fidelity to the best of your convictions is the focus of this Bud-ism.

Faithful to Self

As you have read through this book and hopefully have taken time to reflect upon and perhaps enact the various Bud-isms, perhaps you have uncovered that which is unique and special about yourself. Perhaps you have even rekindled a number of buried dreams, visions, or desires about how to be and how you wish to live your life. Well, now is the time to commit. Commit to yourself to allow this new self-awareness and awakened sense of purpose guide your decisions. Be faithful to this authentic you.

- First, ask yourself what is it that you discovered that you wish you had done or continued to pursue? Write it down. Place a reminder in your calendar or on the refrigerator to do it. It is not too late so, do it, *now!*

- What is it that you find yourself doing out of habit which really doesn't serve your authentic self? If it is not you, then surrender it.

Faithful to Life Values

What do you value? Perhaps it is gentleness, or honesty, or respect. What is it in life that you hold dear, that you cherish? Is it the beauty of nature, the love of another, the freedom to choose? Make a list of the qualities of person and the characteristics of life that you hold in esteem. Make a list of those qualities that you feel make life worth living. Now ask yourself:

- Would others be able to identify these life values simply by oberving how you choose to live your life?

- Do you find yourself a fickle lover of these values—sometimes faithful and sometimes not?

- Does your list truly reflect that which *you* value—or is it merely a listing of nice ideas—things one *should* value?

Challenge Yourself!

If they are *your* life values then they will be reflected in *your* life choices. So commit to embody each of these every day. Commit to be faithful to your values. Commit to finding expression of them in your daily choices.

Not only will this make you faithful to your own desired way of living, but you will show the world what you see IS what you get!

Section IV:
Celebration

*All animals except man know that the principle
business of life is to enjoy it.*

—Samuel Butler

Have you ever stopped and really observed dogs going about their business? As I watch Bud dig in that very special hiding place for his prized bone, he has a singularity of purpose. I call and he ignores me. He appears to be on a mission. Even the cat walking by elicits no more than a momentary glance. Bud is focused on the prize and the prize is DIGGING! Inconveniences of hardened soil, snow cover, or even aging muscle and bones seem to be little deterrents to his purpose. Digging is the business at hand, and digging he will do.

But it is not his singularly of purpose that catches my attention. It is his approach to this "business" of his life. His scratching, digging, and dirt moving appear less like dreaded work and more like activity of joy and celebration. It seems reminiscent of watching children "working" hard to open birthday gifts.

His enthusiasm doesn't appear dampened by the size of the bone, the ease of digging, nor his desire for someone else to dig for him. He doesn't appear overwhelmed by the other things on his "to do" list.

Actually, the closer I observe the more I realize that Bud really is *not* engaged in work, nor business. Bud is simply being. He is simply a bone-burying-Bud at that moment. It is his current state of life, and he appears to enjoy every moment of it.

We, however, too often busy ourselves with so many "to do's" that we have little time "to be." Too often we see the business of life as a deterrent to living. You know how it goes: I will relax, I will enjoy my life *when*... I retire; I complete my work; tomorrow; etc.

I know there are times when I look around me and only see the bills, or the weeds in the garden, or the other caterpillars in my life, all to the exclusion of the butterflies. Too often my focus is on all that I have to do before I can ever relax and enjoy. But if I am learning anything by watching Bud, and trying to *gain a leash on life*, it is that life, with all of its "caterpillars," life is still meant to be celebrated. I know that the oh, so many tasks to be completed can still be approached and completed within the context of a life to enjoy. This day is life—it's not a dress rehearsal!

George Santayana observed, "There is no cure for birth and death save to enjoy the interval." What a truth! Life is terminal. So why do we squander a single moment fretting about our lives when it is there for us to make the best of, to enjoy, and to celebrate?

I have had occasion to see people in my private clinical practice who are very unhappy with their station in life. Perhaps it is a job that they have done for twenty years that gives them absolutely no joy or satisfaction. Or maybe it is the fact they are in college when that was never exactly what they wanted to do. While I feel sad when I hear of these situations, I am saddened more once I hear their solutions.

Too often these individuals express that things will be okay sometime in the distant future. They say things like, "I only have three more years to graduate," or "If I can stick it out 14 more years, then I get a full pension." And then, I wonder? If you haven't learned how to make the best of *this* moment, why should we assume you will with the next?

Sadly, for too many people, "Life, as it is called, is... one long postponement." (Henry Miller).

Don't let that be true for you. Don't wait until there is a perfect time, or for after all the work is completed, or for the problems to be resolved before you celebrate your life. *Now* is the time to live and celebrate your life. *Now* is the time to open that bottle of wine, or use the fancy china, or simply go out and play and enjoy. It's okay. This IS the business of life!

The lessons that follow—lessons on Play, Marking, and Love—are all lessons that will point the way to making *the principal business of your life to enjoy it!*

Dog-ma 11:
The Dog-ma of Play

The dog was created specially for children.
He is the god of frolic.

—Henry Ward Beecher

It has been suggested (at least once?) that perhaps I am a bit of a workaholic. The grand observers who attempt to point this out note that I am a full professor at the university and I write books and journal articles and I have a private clinical practice where I do therapy and provide consultation services; I also move trees, build stone walls, move mountains, build damns (sorry the last two were just to see if you were paying attention!). Anyway, I do get their point, and there probably is some truth in what they say. Perhaps I do spend too much time doing these tasks as opposed to all of the things I suggested that you do in the preceding chapters. But I'm working on it! And, I have Bud as a constant reminder and invitation.

In fact, today was a great example. I was up early as my body rhythms seem to demand. After making some coffee and opening a window for the morning breeze, I gathered my notes and sat at the computer to begin my writing. I wasn't particularly inspired but my "rule" is that I will sit and try to write something and hope inspiration follows. Well, I had been sitting for some time and inspiration must have hit the snooze alarm. So I sat... I reviewed notes... I wrote a few lines and then all of a sudden, out of nowhere, came this barking. I banged my knee on the desk it startled me so much. As I turned holding my knee, I saw Bud. The dog is nuts. He was sitting in the doorway to my office. He barked, stood, sat, barked. Then he ran down the hall, came back, barked and ran back down the hall. By now I figured that he had seen one too many Lassie movies and was trying to tell me Timmy was in the well. Anyway, I got up to see if something was wrong and what did I find? A clothes basket. Clean clothes! And inside the basket? Bud! No Timmy, no well, nothing wrong. Just a 14-year-old dog acting like a pup and wanting to play. What a great friend he is. What a model of health he can be!

Being a product of what has been called a "Protestant (although I am Catholic) work ethic," I often find that I need an excuse to play. You know: "Well, I work very hard all week, I deserve to have some time off on the

A god of frolic.

weekend!" or "I just completed the manuscript... Now I can celebrate!" I can hear Shakespeare now: "I pray you... your play needs no excuse. Never excuse." But for me and perhaps for you, being playful, especially now that we are "responsible" adults, often requires if not an excuse, at least an explanation. Doesn't it?

No! It really doesn't. And, the Bud-ism that follows invites you to come out to play. No excuses and no explanations needed. Just celebration!

A Bud-ism: Lessons on Play

One of my dearest friends and a co-author on a number of the books I have written once called me to task on my "need to play later." We had just completed a trip to New York City where we signed a contract for a new book. On the train ride back home, Bob started to plan a playful weekend of celebration. I tried to dampen his enthusiasm by saying, "Bob, it's just a contract. We have to write the book first and then let's *really* celebrate." And in his most therapeutic, Woody Allen voice, he responded, "Hmmmmm. What a wonderful idea! *Really* celebrate when we finish the book. I like it! In fact, I'll take it. Yep, I'll take it and add it to let's celebrate the signing of the contract. Then let's celebrate a bit more... sending the first draft... and then getting the artwork for the cover... and then receiving the proofs... and then having the manuscript in our hands... and then..." I got his point.

You don't need an excuse to play, nor to celebrate. You may just need a Bud or a Bob in your life to remind you and to invite you to play (at least until you learn how to invite yourself).

Make Room for Play by Doing Nothing

Bud knows there are times to eat, to sleep, to do his "work" digging, and time to chase squirrels and absorb his world. But he also seems to appreciate that "Work is not always required... there is such a thing as sacred idleness..." (George MacDonald). Yes, Bud can certainly exemplify "sacred idleness"—and do so without any signs of guilt.

When was the last time you *allowed* yourself to do nothing? I don't mean those times when your work was completed and you had a lull between projects, a lull that you most likely were frenetically trying to figure out how to fill. NO. When was the last time you really allowed yourself to do nothing? Maybe now is the time to develop your ability to embrace idleness. To relish doing nothing!

If you are walking on the beach, walk not for exercise nor to treasure hunt—walk simply as an alternative to standing. Be open and aware of that which presents itself. Or, if you are sitting outside, do so without purpose. Sit, not with the purpose of clearing your mind or of taking a nap, or of gathering some "rays" (all of course can happen). Sit, if even for a few moments, to simply allow what happens to happen.

Now I need to caution you. If you are like me, then doing nothing will be quite a challenge. In fact, you may even be tempted to make "doing nothing" into a project! Please don't! The task is simply to allow yourself to embrace the truth that the sacred can sometimes be found in our idleness—if we will allow it.

Playing Hookey... The First Step

I grew up in Pennsylvania where some of my fondest school day memories were of waking with my alarm, only to find that through the night the earth became blanketed with snow. These were mornings where my eyes would pop wide and my heart would begin to race.

I would leap from bed and dash downstairs. The enthusiasm exhibited was not in anticipation of seeing the white blanket of snow out my front door. No, this arousal was in hopes of hearing the T.V. announce our school closing!

What a grand gift: my work had been cancelled *and* I had nothing planned.

When was the last time you took a snow day... or a mental health day... or simply played hookey? I am not referring to those times when you took off work to do some needed chores, or finish other projects. No, I am asking about unplanned holidays. When was the last time that you found your day free of "have to's" and without an agenda—a day with an empty "to do" pad.

If it has been too long since you've experienced this freedom to play, then let me suggest that you go out an rent the movie *Ferris Bueller's Day Off*. After watching the movie open your calendar (or better yet ask a dear friend to do it for you) and then, blindly flip to any date and write in big, bold letters SNOW DAY! When the calendar opens to that page, do it! Take it off! The world won't end. There's a ball game calling your name, or a romp in the clean laundry basket—or even a snow man to build! So go and have fun!

Release the Child Within

Watching Bud in the laundry basket reminded me of his days as a pup—days when he would carry a clean sock into the family room just to have someone tug on it and play. That puppy—both then, and the puppy within him now—are certainly "gods of frolic." The same could be said of the child within you!

I can remember times at Christmas when my children would open their gifts, especially those neat little kid gifts of race cars, Legos, even playmobile and I would sit with them and play (like a good father should). What the world didn't know was that I *was playing!* The kids were just my excuse. Somehow, I felt better having permission as an adult to play with childish toys and games.

What are your toys? When was the last time you really played with them? When was the last time you treated yourself to a new one?

Maybe it is that old train set that you set up as decoration for Christmas. Why wait until Christmas? Now is a good time to play with the trains? Or maybe you have a wonderful collection of stuffed bears, or china dolls, that are exquisitely arranged and displayed throughout your house. Why not take them down, touch them, remember how and when and where you got them. Place them in other spots throughout the house so that they can see your world from a new angle and you can include them in more of your daily perspective.

And your play doesn't need to be restricted to your possession and use of toys. "And forget not that the earth delights to feel your bare feet and the winds long to play with your hair." (Kahil Gibran)

When was the last time you let your toes be tickled by the grass, your face refreshed by a gentle rain, and your hair re-styled by a playful wind. Why not?

Go ahead—walk in the woods and return the songs of the birds and the "hello's" of all its inhabitants.

Go ahead—go out in the next gentle rain and play in it; dance as if no one is watching.

Go ahead—rest in the sun and be renewed by its warmth and identify the many creatures, characters, and things the clouds can become.

And, if you really are ready, find that wonderful grassy hill that beckons you to roll down its slope!

Having made the room (doing nothing) and time (playing hookey), you now can invite your child to play, and in so doing you will come to understand as our dogs already do, "that the principle business of life is to enjoy it."

Dog-ma 12:
The Dog-ma of Marking

If I have any beliefs about immortality,
it is that certain dogs I have known will go
to heaven and very, very few persons.

—James Thurber

I guess the hope of living beyond death, if not in body at least in spirit, is felt by all of us, especially as we find ourselves more deeply rooted in our adult years! The apparent strength and universality of this need to be remembered—to leave our mark—to live on in another is poignantly depicted by Richard Bode in his book, *Beachcombing at Miramar.* On one excursion he observed a "note" etched in the wet sand and then another from a second author, further down the beach... and yet another and another. Notes, each reflecting something unique about its author and each as testimony to their presence on the shore line. The last note was that which, for me, was the most profound and descriptive of our human condition. The unassigned testament stated simply "I am here!" to which Bode felt compelled to add, "I am here, too."

Leaving our mark, becoming a part of history or leaving personal legacy is our way of achieving immortality, our way of letting all who follow us know that not only were we here, but that we made an impression! We left our mark! Leaving a mark is certainly not something new for Bud—or for any of our four legged friends.

There was a time when Bud and I lived in a small college town. Without the pleasures of a backyard he would wait to take a walk about town, sniffing at all the garden flowers we passed and the trees that line the streets. There was this one property that had a beautiful, well-manicured front yard. Each time we passed this house he would walk through the grass, stop to inhale its aroma, and then with only the slightest indication, he would plop down, roll onto his back and begin to wiggle in the grass. He looked like a baby freely splashing in a bath, or a child rolling, without concern, down a grassy hill. Such joy. Such freedom. Such abandonment. Bud was not only aware of the wonders of the lawn, but was partaking in its wonderful feel and *in return sharing his scent!*

It is hard to know if the grass delighted in this

We all need to leave our mark.

process but there is no doubt, Bud did! There is also no doubt that all of his four legged friends who passed that way that day knew that Bud was there! He left his mark.

It should be obvious at this juncture in the book that Bud's mark, his legacy, extends well beyond the scent he leaves behind. In fact, it is not his impact on the external world that is his legacy at all. It is his impact on my heart and the hearts of all who have encountered him that will remain as his "mark," well after his scent has dissipated.

Leaving our mark—what an interesting concept. What mark, what legacy do you wish to leave? What notation in the history of the world do you hope to make about your presence here, about your uniqueness and your contribution? What imprint on the hearts of those who truly know you do you hope to make? And how do you intend to do this? Perhaps the following lessons from Bud will help you answer these questions and position you to better leave your "mark."

A Bud-ism: Lessons on Marking

When you entered this world, you probably were anything but shy in proclaiming your arrival. You cried and all in ear shot knew you were alive, and they smiled and rejoiced! Yes, you probably made your mark at that point. So, why stop now?

When was the last time you announced you were alive? When was the last time you announced your arrival in a way that all within earshot could smile and rejoice. If it has been awhile, then it's time to start! It is time to make your mark!

Start With a Mini-Marking

If you are in a location where there is a sandy beach, why not write a message, your name, or even leave your foot print so that others patrolling that shore line will, for a brief moment, know "you" exist! If sandy shore-line is not within your geography then why not tack a note, or a picture, to a tree next to a wooded path. Perhaps it will be a hiker, a jogger, a hunter, or even a searcher of truth that discovers that note and in so doing discovers part of you. If this book finds you in a winter season, perhaps a special snow creation can be your signature? Make something ephemeral, something creative, something *you!*

Now With a Little More Gusto and a Bit More Permanence

Rather than sea-side sand or snow-based creations, why not disturb that newly leveled cement with a hand print or your initials? Or maybe you could find an old and somewhat lonely tree stump simply waiting for your markings! Why not place the pronouncement of your love, your dreams—of you—on that receptive tree so that the next to travel that way will know you were there?

Expanding the Message

Perhaps, as you journeyed through this book you discovered or re-discovered what you truly value in life. Why not find a way to symbolize these values, beliefs, and insights. Write them down, or gather things that represent them (pictures, artifacts, creations, etc.). Now, find a suitable and deserving container in which to house them. Perhaps you can create a special keepsake box, one containing a special sea shell, or a locket of your baby's hair?

With your own creativity and style make a time capsule of your precious thoughts, memories, hopes and dreams, and lived values. Find a fitting spot for these to be placed in safe keeping, only to be discovered at some later date.

Just perhaps on some future dig an excavator will discover these artifacts and upon reflection of the discovered treasure know that there was a "you" who walked this way!

More Than Just Things

It has been said that "Immortality lies not in the things you leave behind, but in the people your life has touched" (Author unknown).

So, each of the above suggested activities are but a beginning to your marking. They are only the first steps toward leaving your legacy and creating your immortality. Real immortality, real legacy comes not from the "what" we leave behind, but from the "who" we have touched.

Now is a good time to revisit, by way of reflection and memory, all who have joined with you in your journey. Remember the many who have traveled at least part of the way.

Remember those who made their mark *on* you! Those whose presence in your life left you better for it. A teacher? A coach? A family member or mentor?

Remember them, remember what they mean to you, how they have helped give form to you and then tell them! Tell these others of their import in your life and in so doing help continue their legacy, while at the same time beginning your own.

Remember those who sought your council, your support, or simply your companionship at a time when each of these were needed. It is in their hearts that your mark has become indelible! Remember them and again reach out to them and ask them how you have impacted their life. Share how important they are in yours. Thank them for the privilege of being part of their journey.

Asserting Your Presence is Ongoing

Marking is not just about yesterday. Look about you. Who is it that now walks with you and joins you in this phase of your journey? Who is it that follows? A brother or sister? A younger friend? A nephew or niece—your own son or daughter!

What is that you wish them to know and remember about you? By what do you want to be remembered? Will it be a smile? A hug? Your availability? Your frequent words of support and encouragement?

Whatever it is, reach out and make contact. Send a card, an email, or a letter to them explaining what they have given to you and your life and offering them that which is yours to share.

Perhaps you are fortunate to have, or will have, achieved much—acquired much—and have many things to point to as a sign of your success. But all of these will perish. All of these markings will fade. Just as surely will the tide rise and wash away the markings of those who walked on the beach. However, touching another's heart is what poems are written about is why lyrics are sung, and stories passed down from generation to generation. Make a commitment to live your life in a way that it becomes a poem, a song, a story of a life celebrated. Commit to sharing "you" and not simply "yours"—and in so doing, touch the lives and the hearts of others.

Now, that's a mark. One that will live on, well after you are gone.

Dog-ma 13:
The Dog-ma of Love

I talk to him when I'm lonesome like,
And I'm sure he understands.
When he looks at me so attentively,
and gently licks my hands;
Then he rubs his nose
on my tailored clothes,
but I never say naught...,
For the good Lord knows I can buy more clothes,
but never a friend like that!

—W. Dayton Wedgefarth

It's hard to withdraw from bud—either through anger, self-absorption, or any other such barrier to love. He won't let you. Yes, the pants were just cleaned and his nose still had the remnants of burying that bone, but all he wants is to touch and be touched. All he wants is to share himself. All he wants is to love.

Sharing self, sharing love, even when it comes at the "cost" of another cleaning bill, is wonderful. But loving is more than just wonderful. It is essential. In his book,

Teachings on Love, Thich Nhat Hanh writes, "Without love, life is impossible."

Each of us has a calling—a calling to love. It is innate. It is a calling that is not restricted to that one special person or soul mate, but is meant to be the calling to a way of life, a way of living, a way of being. This is a lesson that our four legged friends appear to have learned.

> "I think dogs are the most amazing creatures; they give unconditional love. For me they are the role model of being alive." (Gilda Radner)

Role models for unconditional loving; role models for being alive!—Wow, quite a statement! Yet, my own experience with one "grand-master of loving" Bud, certainly affirms Gilda's observation, at least for me. Bud most certainly gives me so many signs of his love; he does not ration it out nor distribute to me only at those times or on those occasions where I've done something special for him. Further, his love is NOT contingent on my feeding him, patting him, or providing him with treats. In fact, not only doesn't he make his love contingent on what I do for him, it is not even restricted to me! He is just as loving to others he has

Grand-master of love.

come to know. It is his special way of being, unconditionally loving.

So what is this unconditional loving that seems to be so deeply needed and yet so oftentimes absent? Is it that which is portrayed so passionately in story and song? Is it that which is reflected in Hallmark cards?

This unconditional love is not tied to occasion or conditions. It is a love that is not just of body or of mind; it is a love that is of the spirit and being. It is an overwhelming sense of connectedness and a subsequent valuing of that connectedness. It is the valuing of another, not because of what that other has (money, prestige, beauty), or does (achieves, supports, encourages), but valuing and prizing of another, regardless of these conditions, and embracing them just because they are in your life.

Unconditional love is what you experience when you stand outside the large glass window in a hospital nursery, looking in at those recent miracles of birth adorned in blue and pink caps and blankets. As you look upon these new additions to our human family, you know what it means to look beyond, or behind, the conditions of these "bundles of joy" and truly prize them as they are. Specifics of gender, ethnicity, or family background really don't matter. It doesn't really matter how they are dressed, or how they are acting. Looking at those newborns, at these early moments of life, touches something deep within us, something that stirs a warmth, a joy, that is natural and unconditional—that is love.

Sadly, too often our ability to love this way is inhibited. It is blocked by our tendency to hold out our love as a prize to be won or earned rather than something that needs to be given freely. To love in this way requires us to look beyond the conditions of another—beyond "conditions" such as appearance, manner of presentation, background, even actions—and simply value the fundamental person behind these conditions.

It is essential that we continue to learn to touch that love within and allow it to give shape to all of our life choices. This, of all the lessons, may be the one most important and most essential for us to learn.

A Bud-ism: Lessons on Love

As I watch Bud it becomes so very clear that while he has the rules of territoriality and the script of dog-chase-cat deeply ingrained, he also approaches his world with what appears to be reverence. When introduced to a puppy, he lowers his head and approaches slowly. There seems to be no need to dominate; rather, he allows the pup to sniff and even snip. And, when approached by an eager human toddler, he seems to know that a tug here and a yank there will soon be coming, but he waits and endures.

While I'm not sure that Bud "sees" Divinity in all forms of life, he certainly acts in ways that seem to demonstrate an "honor" for it.

All too often, we fail to show honor, reverence, and love for that which is in our world. Our culture often-times encourages us to view life as cheap, easily discarded in this throw-away culture of easy divorce, abandoned or neglected children, and cruelty to animals and nature—all signs of the absence of love. And this absence can't be attacked or fought. Rather, it is an absence that needs to be filled with love for self, others, and all of creation.

Love as Reverence

Our first lesson of love is to approach life, in all of its forms, with reverence. So during this coming week...

- Smile at a stranger or colleague, a smile of recognition. Smile in a way that conveys your awareness that they, just like you, are simply co-journeying in this life, with neither being more valuable than the other.

- Offer your seat to one less able to stand, or allow another to pass through the door or enter the elevator before you. Simple acts, yet when done with a reverent heart can express care, connectedness, and love.

- Go to a hospital nursery and spend 10 minutes studying the wonderful faces, tiny hands and feet of all these newcomers to our world. Become completely aware of the power of this miracle of life. And as you pause in front of these new creations, ask yourself, as a living being... Are you really more valuable than any of these?

Loving All You Do

"Only the heart knows how to find what is precious." (Fyodor Dostoyevsky)

Have you listened to your heart recently? Before you become too entangled or enmeshed in your daily activities, take a moment, quiet and reflective, to listen to your heart. What in your world makes you smile? What in your daily experiences is reason to celebrate and exclaim the value of this day? Now...

- Select the blouse, sweater, shirt, tie, ribbon, or pin— the article to wear today this is not simply something that you like, but something with special memory, special meaning, special love.

- If going out, leave a little earlier than usual. Travel a route that may not be the straightest or the most time-efficient way toward your destination, but is the one that provides you sights, sounds, and opportunities to reflect on those aspects of your life that you love.

- As you approach your work—be it within the home, or outside—identify one task to perform, and embrace it with all the gusto you can manage. It is *your* work, so, put *you* into it. Take pride in what you are doing as if you will sign this work of art—as a testimony to you, your abilities, your talents and passion.

- Approach those with whom you spend part of your day and in some way—with a simple gesture or word—let them know that they are more than simply a "like" in your life. Let them know that they are a "love."

Love as Relationship

A person that seeks relationship only to gratify his or her own needs is not in a loving relationship; in fact, it is not even truly a relationship. It is an arrangement, one failing to respect the uniqueness and value of those involved. It is an arrangement of service. Once the utility of the other ceases to exists, so does the need or interest in the arrangement.

Relationships of substance, of depth, are relationships of love. Love as relationship requires understanding, acceptance, and valuing of the other.

Loving an other means you are there for him or her, not just at times of special need but anytime you share a moment in your lives. So as you move forward in your interactions and relationships with those whom you love, check to be sure that you are...

- Present to them—Do you attend to them when they share their day's story? Do you respect their needs, their journey, and honor their invitation for you to join them? Don't allow your own self- absorption to cheat you out of receiving the gift of self that they offer.

- Aware and knowledgeable of them—Do you show an interest in getting to know him/her? Are you active in acquiring this knowledge? Don't wait for their invitation. These "others" are gems waiting to be discovered.

Loving as Giving

What do you give to others—those whom you love? Surely there are the gifts of special occasion and your willingness to assist them at times of need. These are, or can be, acts of love if given from the heart, with the hands serving merely as the vehicle of delivery. But do you give gifts of the heart and loving actions?

- Review the many "gifts" you have provided in the past. How were they chosen? Did the gift you give reflect that which was in your heart? Or merely the limits of what was in your wallet?

- In reviewing those gifts you have provided, consider how were they given. Did you give gifts to win favor, or only in reciprocity, or as a way to establish indebtedness? Or, did you give gifts because the love in your heart simply spilled out into and through your hands?

- While you are most likely very generous with your time, energy and resources, are you equally as generous with sharing of "you."

Through your reading of this book you may have discovered some things about yourself that are new to you. Share that awareness with another. Give those whom you love this newly discovered part of you.

Final Thoughts

Dogs lives are too short. Their only fault, really.

—A.S. Turnbull

Wile we have come to the end of this book, we stand only at the beginning of our lessons. For me, there is so much more to learn about *gaining a leash on life*. For me, there is so much of what I placed in these pages that I need to practice, I need to embrace, I want to embody.

I hope that you have found *Gaining a Leash on Life* to be more than a book. I hope you have experienced these pages as an invitation and a guide to gaining a new perspective. But most of all, I hope that you found the time you spent reading this text to be worthwhile in nourishing your own human spirit.

Throughout the book, I spoke of the wisdom to be gained by observing and reflecting upon my Bud. By now you understand it is not just my Bud—but it is all of the Buds and Baileys, Gus' and Happys, Jakes and Spunkies, who gift our lives. They are our friends. They are our faithful companions. And, if we allow, they can be our own very special teachers.

A.S. Turbull has it right. Dogs lives are too short, especially for one—like me—who is such a slow learner.

A new day, and there is so much more to learn.

About the Author

I know this is an "about me" page but I have to take a moment to place this within its proper context.

I just finished reading the page proofs for the book—and honestly—I am beaming. Andrea Donner, at Willow Creek Press has done a spectacular job and my Illustrator (Ginny Morton), who by the way is also my wife, has truly captured the spirit—the being—of Bud.

So, I sit pretty happy with things—pleased with myself and my work and now begin to draft my "About the Author."

Having written 25 other books, I am pretty familiar with doing this "About the Author" thing. As a result, I was first tempted to simply repeat what I had previously used. So there it was: Name—Richard D., or Richard Dean, or even Rick, Parsons. Then, the significant data: married with five children, three boys, two girls, a graduate school professor... a psychologist, clinician, author, researcher, yada... yada... yada.

So I sit at my desk reading these previous self-disclosures and who steps in to visit me in my office? Bud! Here he is, looking at me, sadly or at a minimum 'questioningly.' It is as if he is saying, "Didn't you read the book?" I believe if he had a voice he would certainly say, "Really, Rick... name, roles, ranks, accomplishments; is this about the Author? Or is this about what the Author does?"

So while Bud is without voice, he is not without communication prowess. So Bud, how's this?

I am a guy who truly believes what I wrote. I have experienced people in my life that actually embrace the dog-mas and Bud-isms presented in this text and are happy, more whole people as a result.

As for me, I'm trying. I believe, but I don't always abide. I understand, but I haven't completely embraced. I'm on my way, but the journey, I pray, will be long and the growth grand. So "About the Author"—he's a guy who tries to live life...

Choosing love...

Choosing joy...

Choosing peace

Choosing patience..., and...

forever—attempting to gain a leash on life.

Rick (and Bud)

August, 2006

About the Illustrator

I am Virginia Morton, a sixth grade science and math teacher. I have longed to spend days with canvas, brush, and the intoxicating fumes of oil and varnish. But, more often, find my dreams directed to the creation of illustrations in my classroom to show viral replication, the water cycle, or number patterns with a white board and dry erase markers.

Working on these illustrations provided me the opportunity to take what has always been a pleasant pasttime and imbue it with purpose. Bud is the perfect muse whether for illustrating or for life. I have never met a dog I didn't like and I believe my three dogs bring me chaos, at times, but more often humility and peace.

Ginny
August, 2006